John Thompson's Modern Course for the Piano | **FIFTH GRADE**

CLASSICAL PIANO SOLOS

19 Original Keyboard Pieces from Baroque to Early 20th Century

COMPILED AND EDITED BY

Philip Low, Sonya Schumann, and Charmaine Siagian

ISBN 978-1-4803-4495-2

WILLIS MUSIC

EXCLUSIVELY DISTRIBUTED BY

HAL•LEONARD® CORPORATION

7777 W. BLUEMOUND RD. P.O. BOX 13819 MILWAUKEE, WI 53213

Visit Hal Leonard Online at
www.halleonard.com

PREFACE

A rarity among piano methods, John Thompson's *Modern Course* was authored by a successful concert artist. For this reason, the pianism found between the pages of the famous "red cover" series corresponds directly with that which is required to play authentic piano literature. A musician of the highest caliber, Thompson (1889–1963) made expert repertoire choices, integrating strong original compositions with accessible arrangements of orchestral and piano classics that perfectly represented the style characteristics of each era, resulting in well-rounded students who could approach any new piece with confidence.

The aim of the *Classical Piano Solos* series is to keep with the spirit of Thompson's repertoire selections by including an assortment of treasured pieces that are taught often and hold status as prized concert music. For example, in the 5th Grade volume are two of the most recognized C-sharp Minor pieces in existence: Beethoven's "Moonlight" sonata and the Rachmaninoff prelude, loved and adored with good reason, yet sometimes unfairly disparaged because of their popularity. (Note that this edition presents the often overwhelming final section of the Rachmaninoff in a more visually accessible layout.) In the same book is Debussy's fast, witty "Doctor Gradus ad Parnassum" and Mozart's D Minor fantasy, unfinished at the time of his death and completed by his student August Eberhard Müller. (Müller's "Lyric Etude" is included in the 1st Grade.) Earlier in the series are other oft-cherished pieces, such as Grieg's spare and wistful "Arietta" and Chopin's intense, evolving "Prelude in E Minor" (both in the 4th Grade), as well as several well-known Bartók miniatures from his 1913 method (1st, 2nd, and 3rd Grade books).

Numerous uncommon treasures were also unearthed, including "A Ghost in the Fireplace" (4th Grade) and "Once Upon a Time There was a Princess" (3rd Grade) from Theodor Kullak's *Scenes from Childhood*, composed for piano students well over a century ago. Though these pieces never quite found their way into published recordings or into the hands of master pianists, for years they provided many students with delightful lesson material as they built their pianistic skills. Other lesser-known gems include works from French composers Mélanie Bonis (*Album pour les tout-petits*, 1st and 2nd Grade) and Cécile Chaminade ("Pièce Romantique," 3rd Grade); Danish composer Ludvig Schytte's Opus 108 (1st and 2nd Grade); Russian composer Anatoly Lyadov's gorgeous, seldom-heard B Minor prelude; and English composer Samuel Coleridge-Taylor's mournful "They Will Not Lend Me a Child," based on a Southeast African folksong about a childless mother (both in the 5th Grade). Quick pieces that dazzle and motivate were intentionally included as well; for example, MacDowell's "Alla Tarantella," C.P.E. Bach's "Presto in C Minor" (both in the 3rd Grade), and Moszkowski's "Tarantelle" (4th Grade).

These authentic piano solos are offered once again in these pages, reconnecting the students of today with beautiful masterpieces from bygone eras.

Correlation with John Thompson's Modern Course. The *Classical Piano Solos* series was compiled to correlate loosely with the *Modern Course* method. The series can be used to supplement any teaching method, but holds its own as a small compendium of advancing piano literature. Worth mentioning is that all the pieces are public domain in the United States, Europe, and around the world. Consequently, no works composed or published after 1920 are included. It is highly recommended that the teacher supplement the lesson with appropriate contemporary literature, including works from outside traditional Western art music, as needed.

Leveling and Layout. Grades 1-4 have been presented in a suggested order of study and progress by approximate level of difficulty. Because of the sophistication and advanced technicality of the pieces in Grade 5, that volume is laid out chronologically, from Baroque to the early 20th Century. Page turns were always a consideration during the engraving and editing process.

Editorial Principles and Sources. When appropriate, occasional articulation, fingerings, and dynamics have been added, especially to pieces from the Baroque and early Classical eras, with the intent of better assisting the advancing performer with an accurate stylistic interpretation. (An exception are fingerings in the Bartók pieces; a few were removed for ease of study.) Urtext sources were consulted whenever available, as well as standard performing editions. The first two pieces in the 1st Grade have been slightly adapted; all other works in the series are originals composed for the keyboard/piano of the time. Compositions without designated titles have been bestowed with fresh ones.

CONTENTS

[It is recommended that at least two contrasting works be learned concurrently]

ORNAMENTATION

In Baroque music, the most frequently used ornament is the *trill* [**tr** or ᰈ], which begins on the auxiliary (less important) note and resolves to the main note. In the Classical, Romantic, and Contemporary periods, the trill typically begins on the main note. In general, ornaments are realized the same way in all periods EXCEPT for the trill. Other common ornaments include the *mordent* [ᰈ] and the *turn* [∾]. See J. S. Bach's neatly written-out ornamentation table and its modern engraving equivalent below.

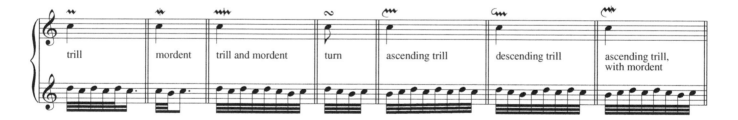

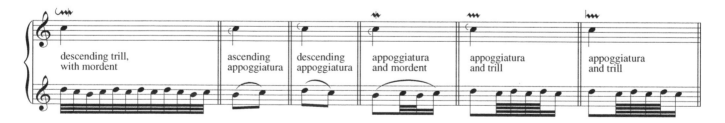

Recommended reading:

Pièces de clavecin (1689) by Jean-Henri d'Anglebert

The Art of Playing the Harpsichord (1716–17) by François Couperin

Essay on the True Art of Playing Keyboard Instruments (1753) by C.P.E. Bach

A Treatise on the Fundamental Principles of Violin Playing (1756) by Leopold Mozart

Introduction to the Art of Playing on the Pianoforte (1801) by Muzio Clementi

Prelude in C-sharp Major

from *The Well-Tempered Clavier* (Book 1), BWV 848

Johann Sebastian Bach
1685–1750

6

Allemande in D Minor

from *Suite in D Minor, HWV 437*

George Frideric Handel
1685–1759

Moderato, cantabile

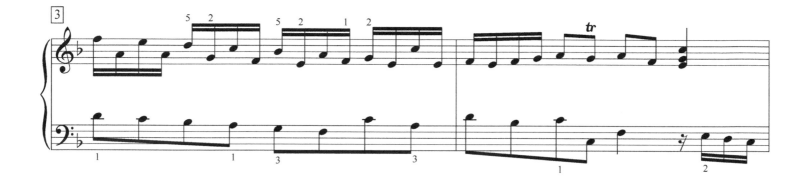

Play eighth notes slightly detached.

Sonata in E Major

K. 531, L. 430, P. 535

Domenico Scarlatti
1685–1757

Play eighth notes slightly detached.

Les niais de Sologne

(The Simpletons of Sologne) from *Pièces de clavecin,* Book 2

Jean-Philippe Rameau
1683–1764

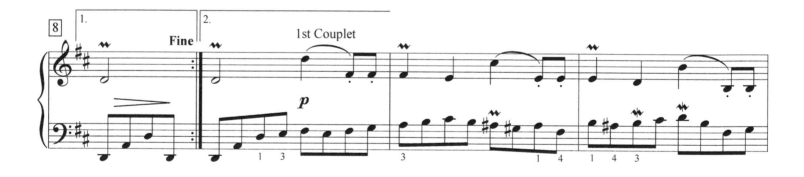

16

1st Double

Rondeau

p

[Play 8th notes ♪♪]

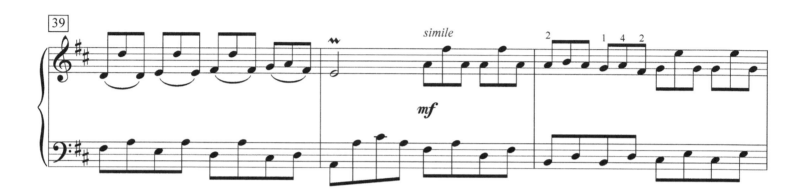

39

simile

mf

42

1st Couplet

f

(2nd time
to 2nd
Couplet)

p

45

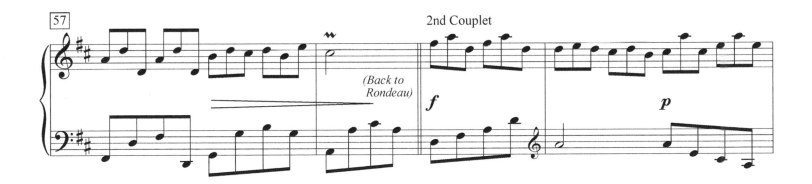

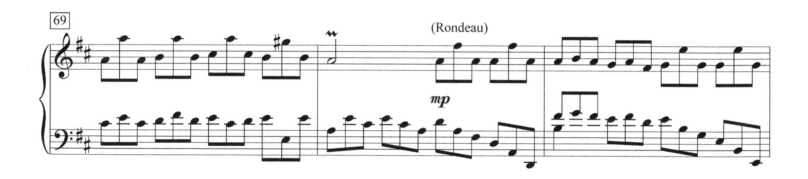

(Rondeau)

Brillante
Rondeau

2nd Double

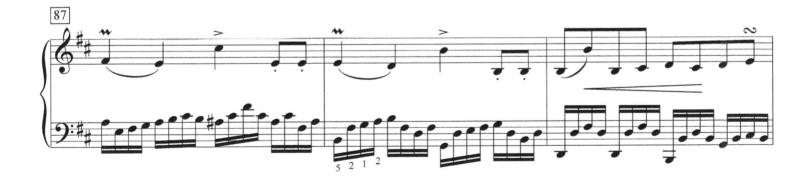

2nd Couplet

(Back to Rondeau)

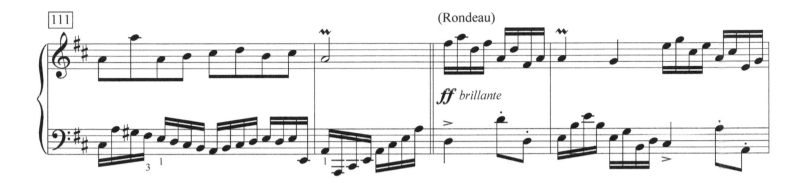

(Rondeau)

Sonata in E-flat Major

Domenico Cimarosa
1749–1801

Andantino

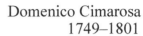

mf espressivo

legato

p

cresc.

f

p

legato

poco cresc.

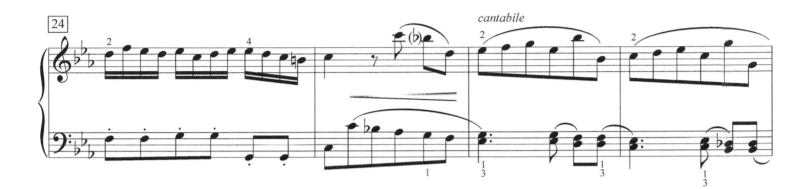

Sonata in D Major
Hob. XVI:4, 1st Mvmt

Franz Joseph Haydn
1732–1809

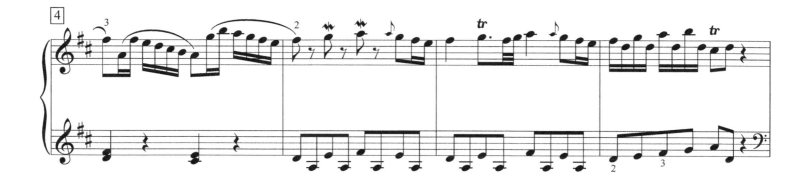

Fantasie in D Minor

K. 397 (posthumous)

Wolfgang Amadeus Mozart
1756–1791

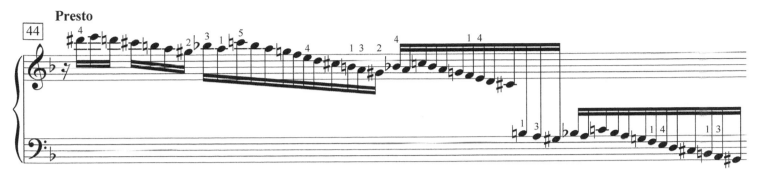

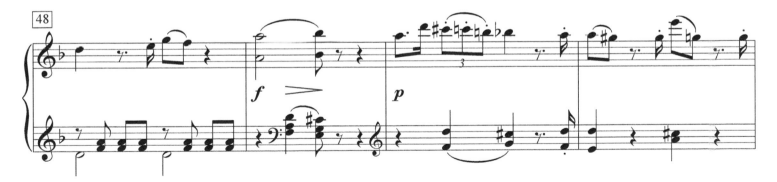

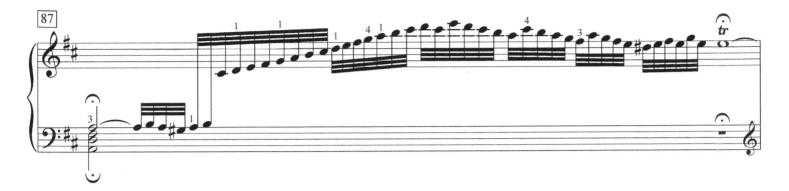

Sonata in C-sharp Minor

Sonata quasi una Fantasia ("Moonlight"), Op. 27, No. 2, 1st Mvmt

Dedicated to Countess Giulietta Guicciardi

Ludwig van Beethoven
1770–1827

*This pedal indication is often questioned. Carl Czerny, a student of Beethoven, believed the composer wanted pedal changes with each new bass note. Other scholars believe he desired a subtle blending of harmonies, achieved on the 19th-century piano by applying the damper pedal continuously from beginning to end. A suggestion for the modern piano: create sympathetic resonance by silently depressing the bottom few notes of the piano, then applying the middle pedal for the duration of the piece.

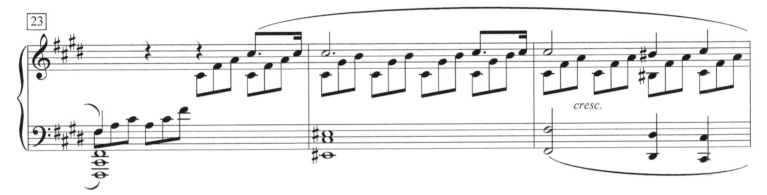

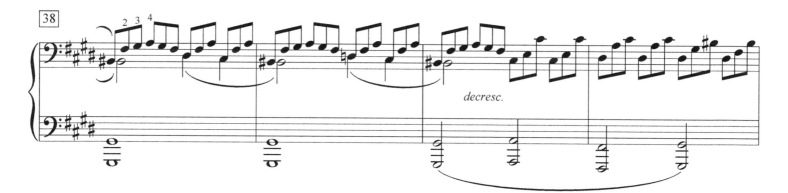

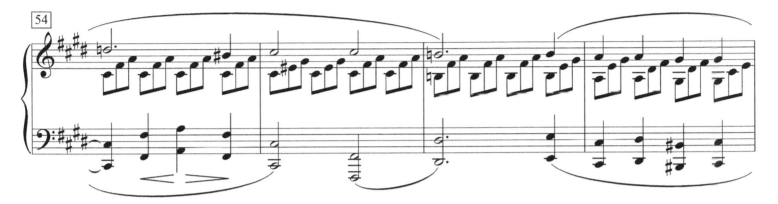

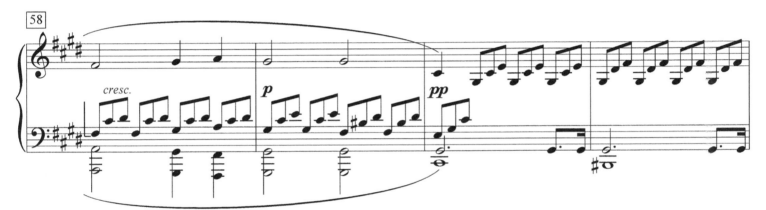

This page has been intentionally left blank to facilitate page turns.

Song Without Words
Op. 30, No. 1

Felix Mendelssohn
1809–1847

Andante espressivo

con pedale

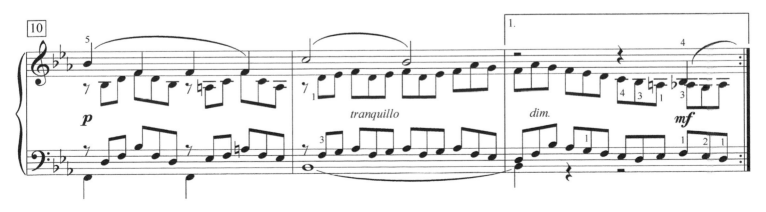

41

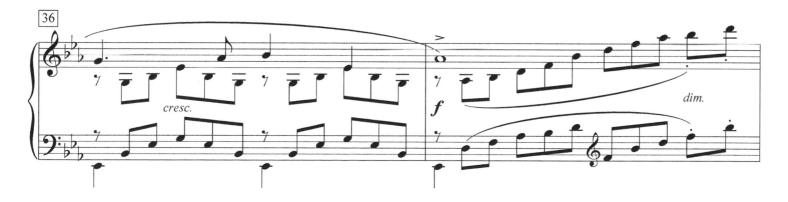

Waltz in A-flat Major

Op. 69, No. 1*

Frédéric Chopin
1810–1849

Tempo di Valse

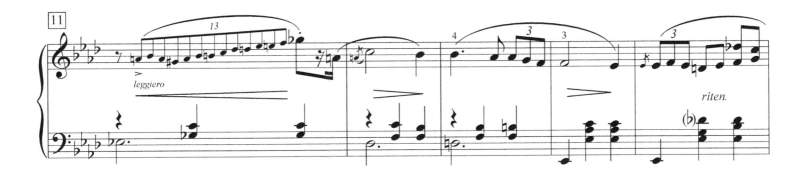

*This edition is based on an autograph dedicated to Elise Peruzzi in 1837. Similar autographs were written for Maria Wodzińska (1835) and Charlotte de Rothschild (1842). A stylized version by Chopin's friend Julian Fontana (published posthumously) is performed most regularly.

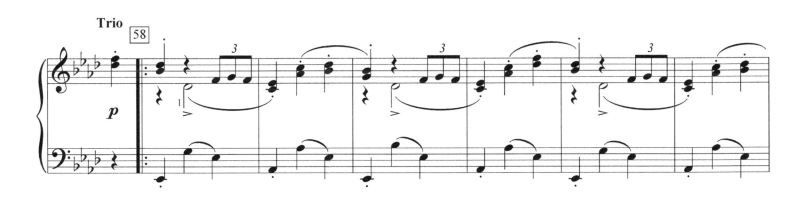

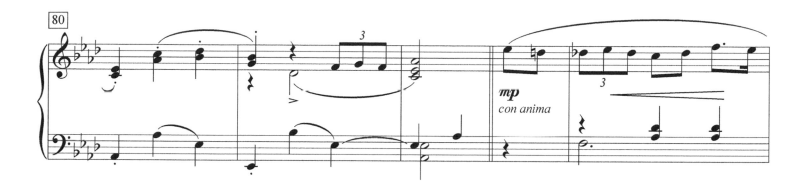

Farewell

(Abschied) from *Waldszenen*, Op. 82, No. 9

Robert Schumann
1810–1856

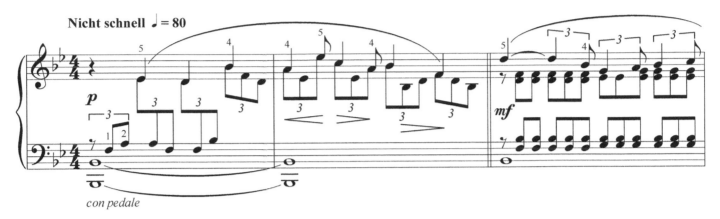

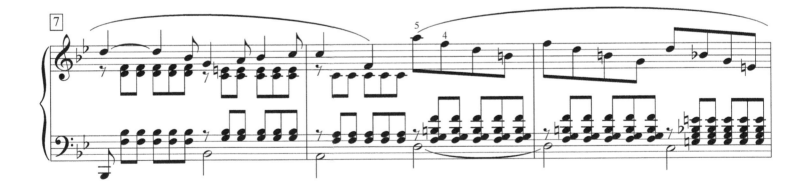

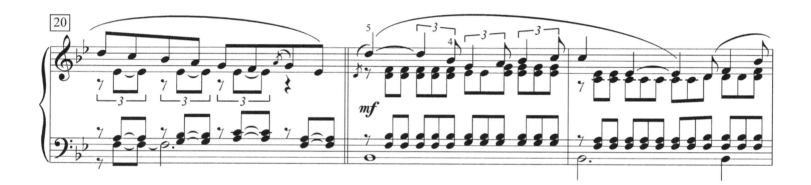

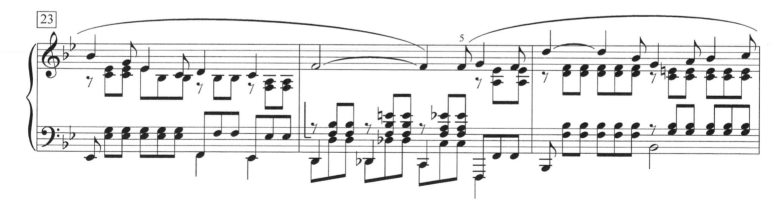

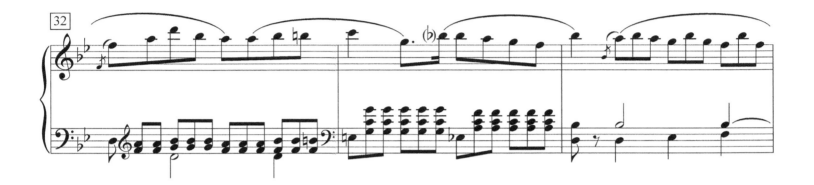

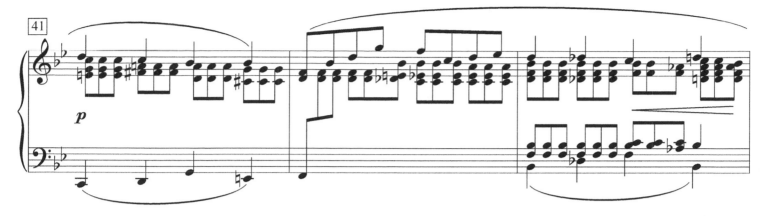

Immer schwächer *(gradually less intense)*

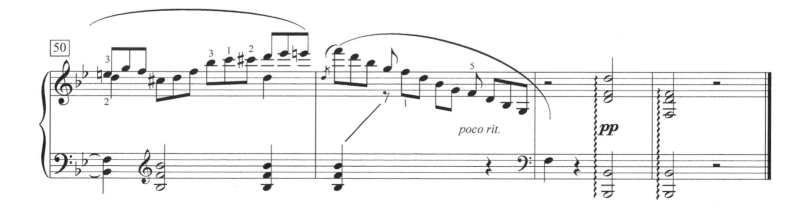

poco rit.

March of the Trolls

(Trolltog) from *Lyric Pieces,* Op. 54, No. 3

Edvard Grieg
1843–1907

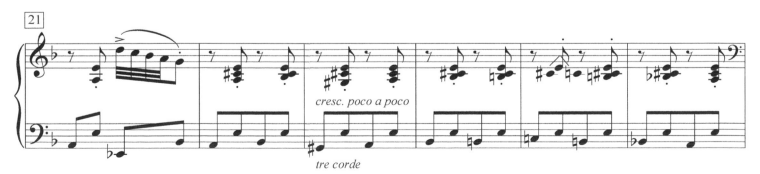

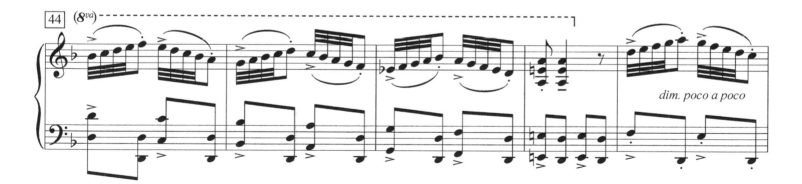

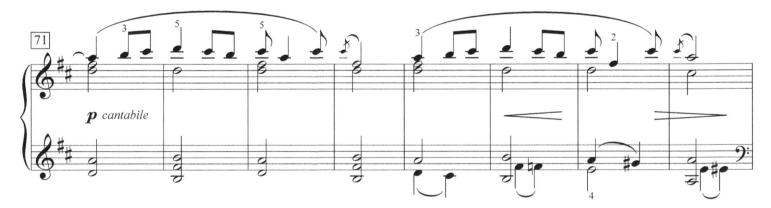

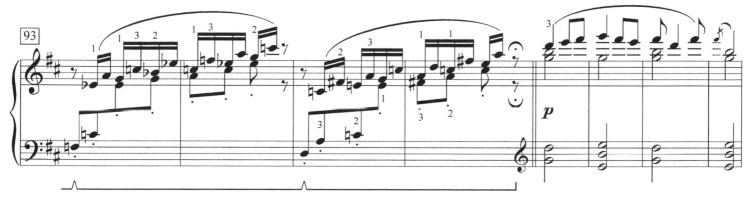

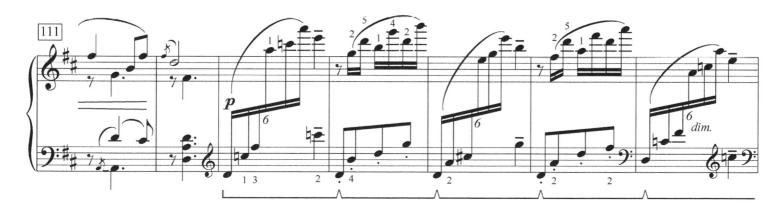

Prelude in B Minor

from *Trois morceaux,* Op. 11, No. 1

Anatoly Lyadov
1855–1914

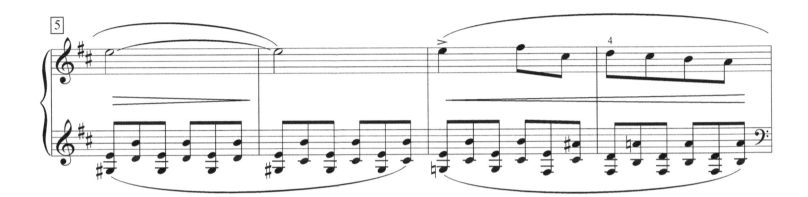

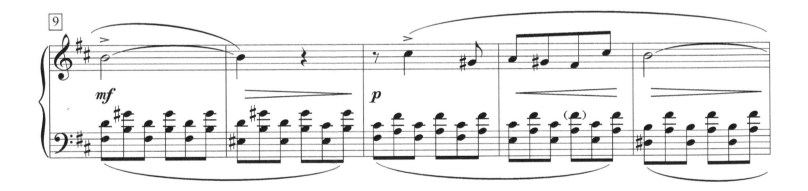

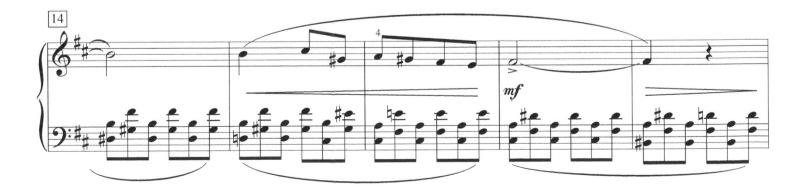

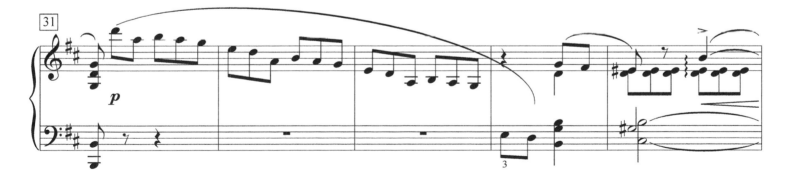

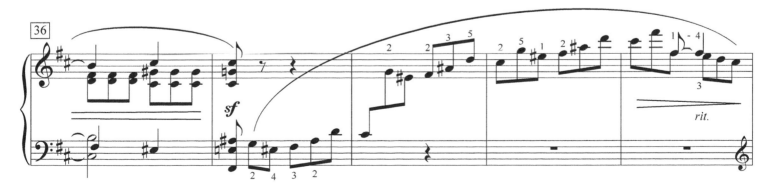

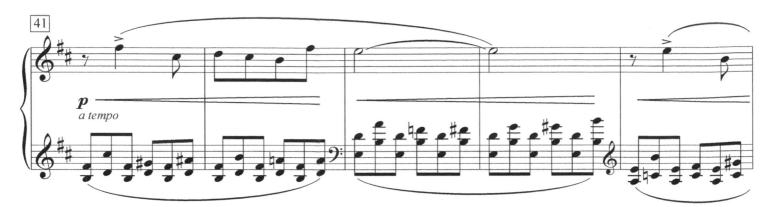

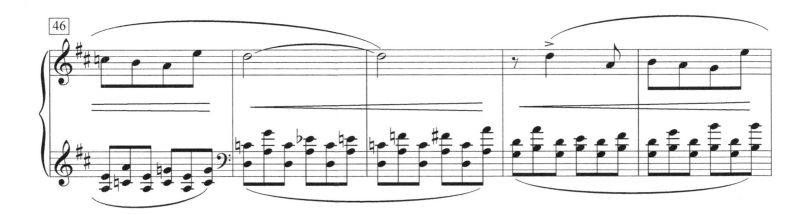

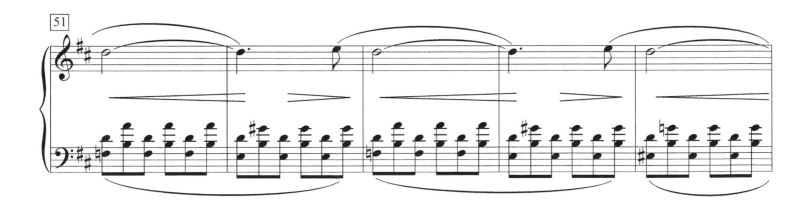

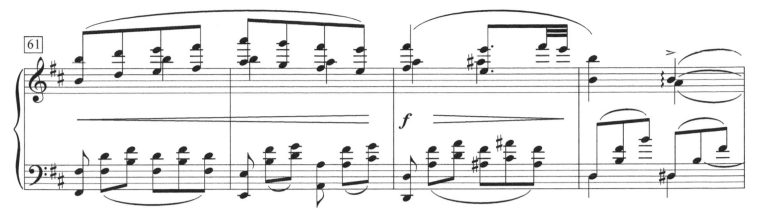

Prelude in D Major

Op. 11, No. 5

Alexander Scriabin
1872–1915

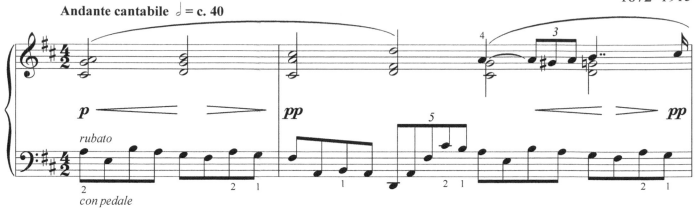

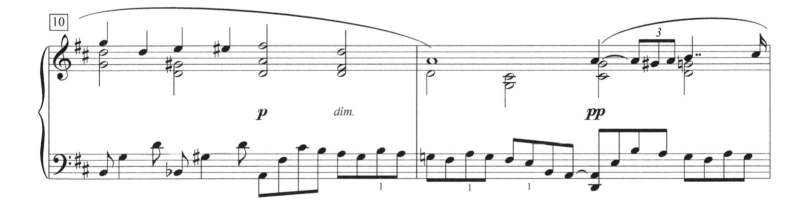

Prelude in C-sharp Minor

from *5 Morceaux de fantaisie*, Op. 3, No. 2

à Monsieur A. Arensky

Sergei Rachmaninoff
1873–1943

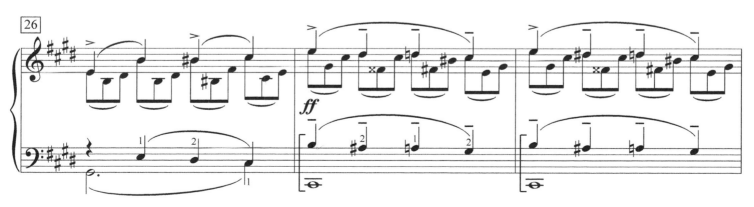

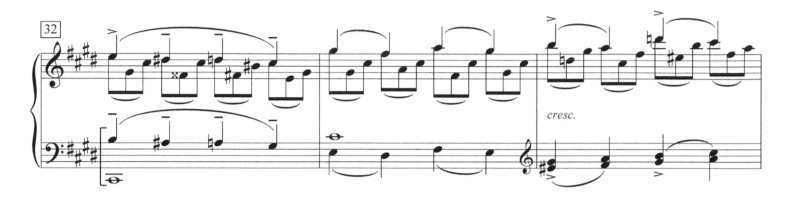

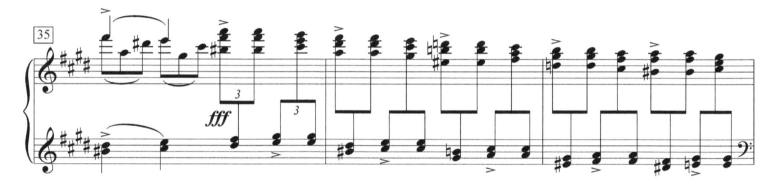

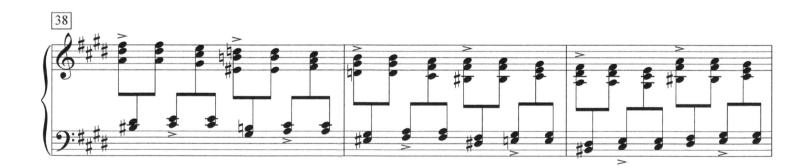

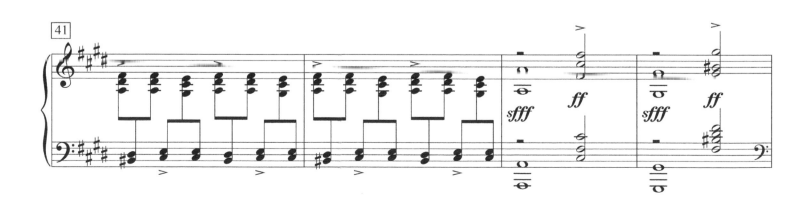

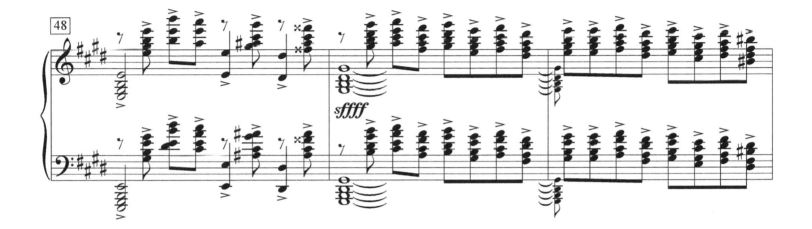

They Will Not Lend Me a Child

Op. 59, No. 4

Samuel Coleridge-Taylor
1875–1912

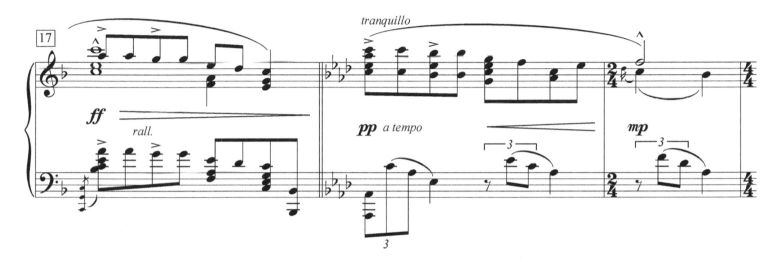

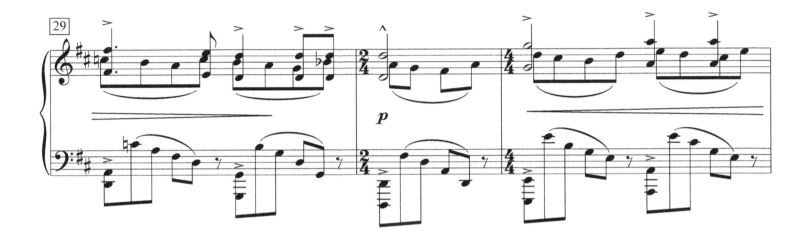

Stick Dance
from *Romanian Folk Dances*, Sz. 56, No. 1

Béla Bartók
1881–1945

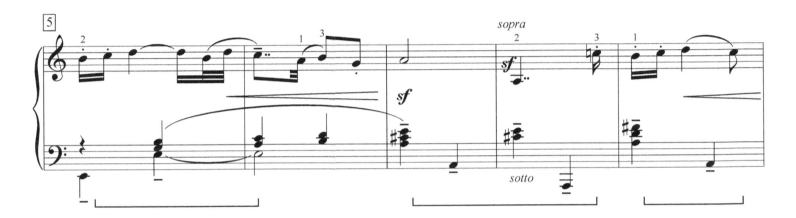

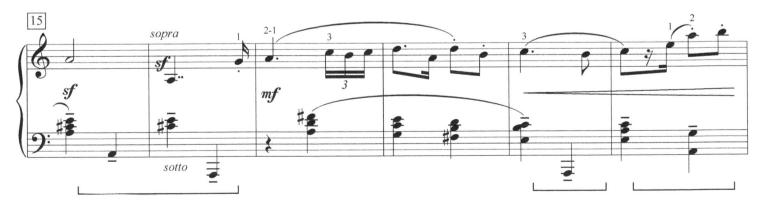

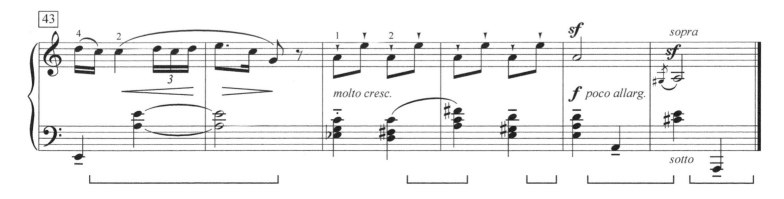

The Lake at Evening

fom *Three Tone-Pictures*, Op. 5, No. 1

To Leslie Hodgson

"...for always...I hear lake water lapping with low sounds by the shore..."
Yeats, *The Lake Isle of Inisfree*

Charles Tomlinson Griffes
1884–1920

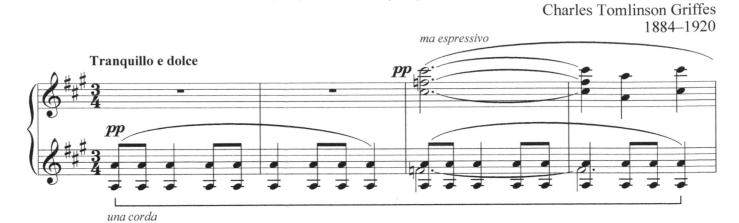

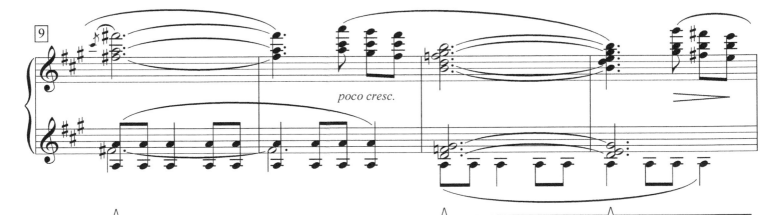

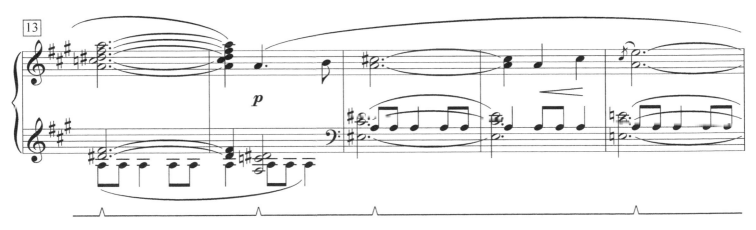

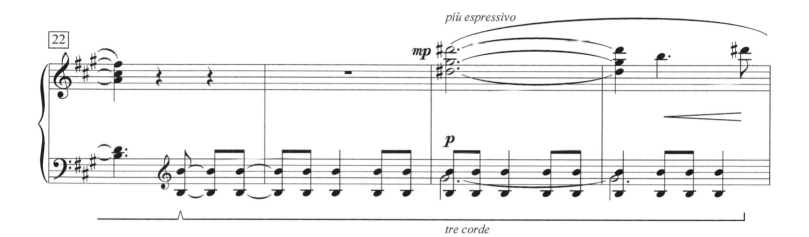

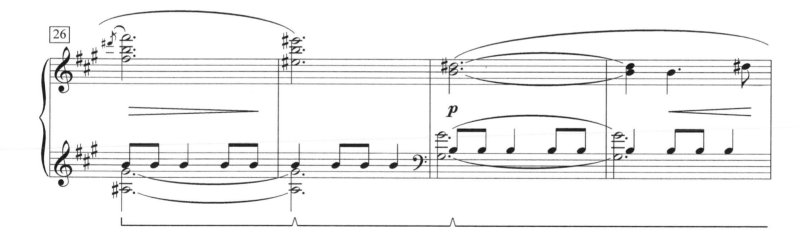

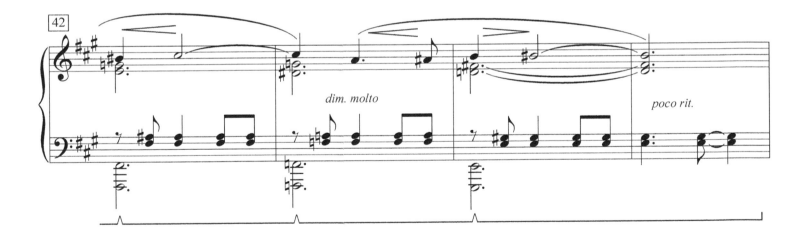

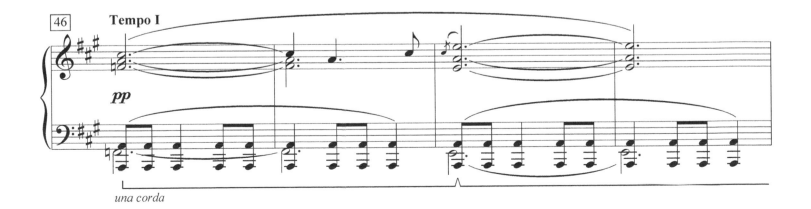

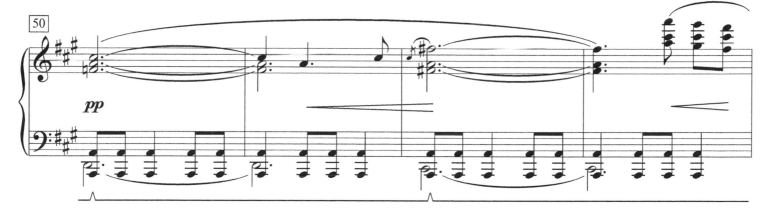

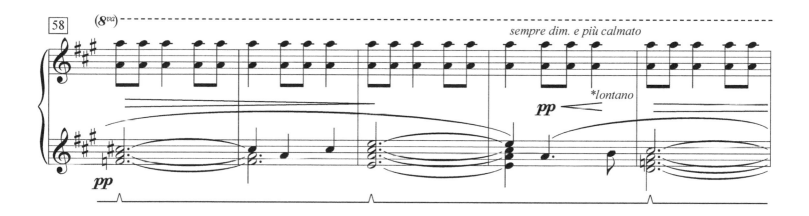

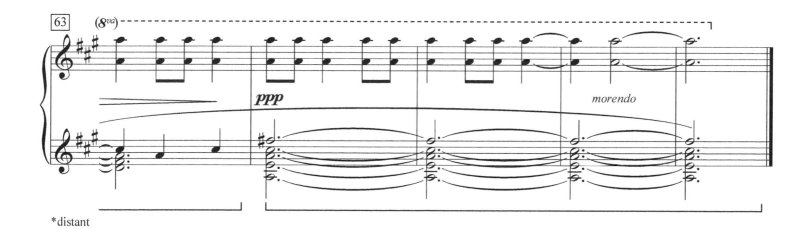

*distant

This page has been intentionally left blank to facilitate page turns.

Doctor Gradus ad Parnassum

from *Children's Corner*

Claude Debussy
1862–1918

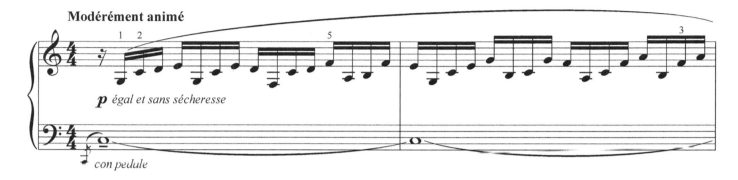

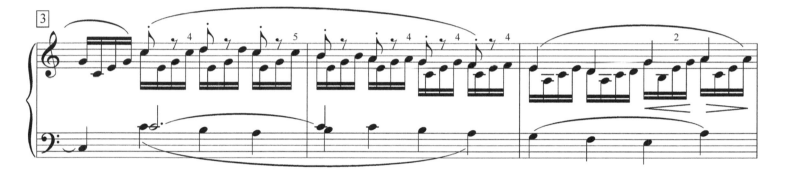

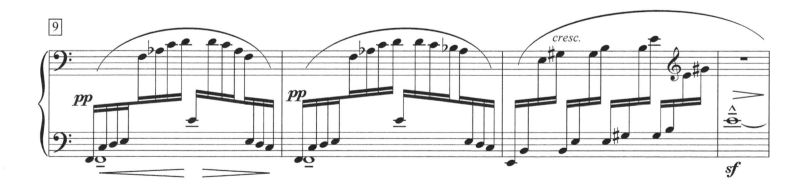

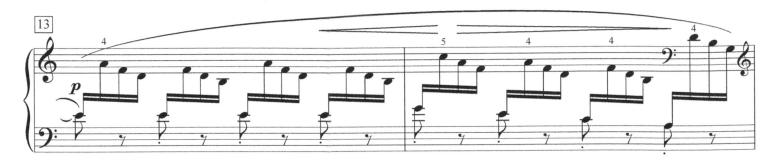

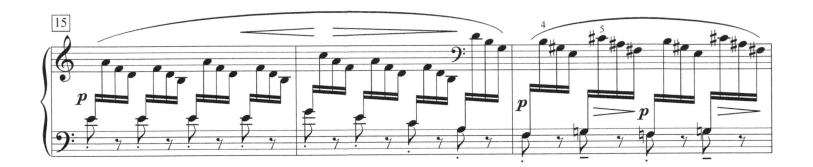

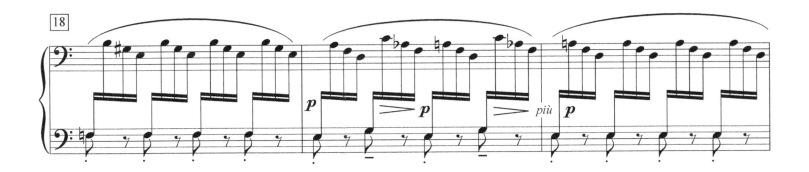

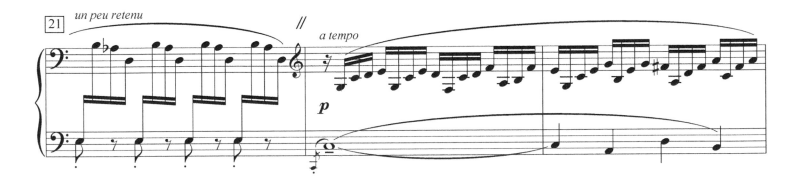

77

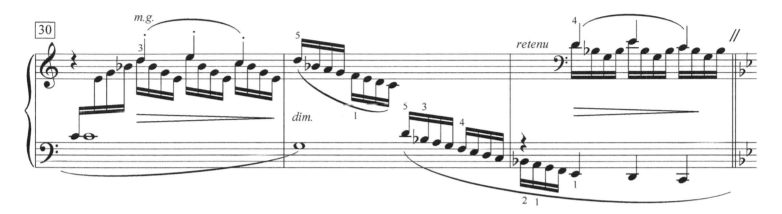

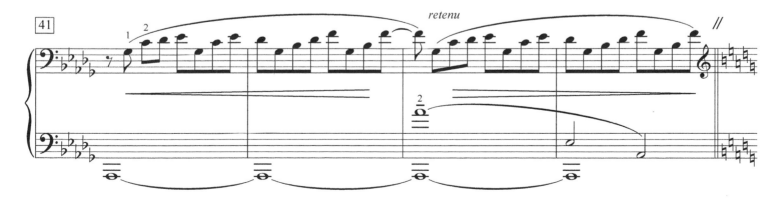

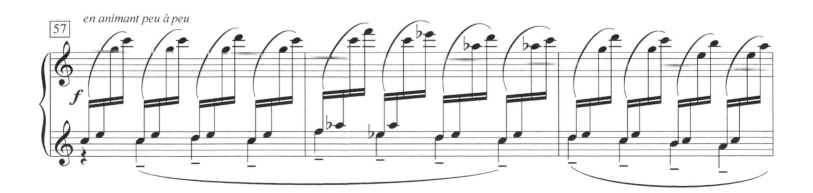

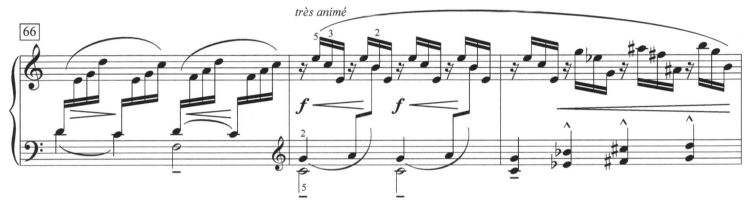

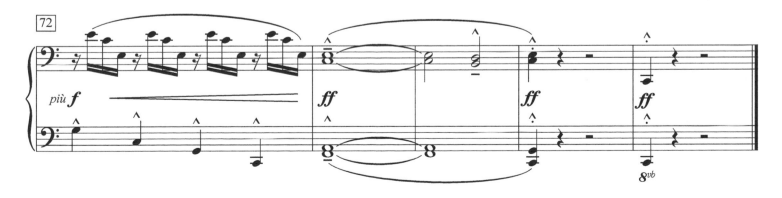

Style characteristics and adjectives that may be helpful when teaching Western keyboard classical music:

BAROQUE (c. 1600-1750) – ornamented, verbose, grand, delicate, decorative, propulsive, embellished, improvisatory, speech-like inflections, counterpoint, binary form, motoric rhythms, drive to the last note of a phrase, the idea of "affections" (each piece has single mood/character).
Major Keyboard Composers: Bach, Handel, Rameau, Scarlatti.

CLASSICAL (c. 1750-1820) – simple, elegant, graceful, natural, melodic, pure, precise, balanced, homophonic (melody with accompaniment), Alberti bass, sonata form, tapered phrases, symmetrical phrases, motivic development, contrasting moods, grace notes played on the beat.
Major Keyboard Composers: Beethoven, Haydn, Mozart.

ROMANTIC (c. 1800-1910) – emotional, dramatic, melodic, *sturm und drang*, flexible, expressive, personal, chromatic, virtuosic, forlorn, nationalistic, programmatic, singing melodies, long gestures, wide leaps, modulations to remote keys, character pieces.
Major Keyboard Composers: Brahms, Chopin, Grieg, Liszt, Mendelssohn, Rachmaninoff, Schumann, Scriabin.

IMPRESSIONIST (c. 1875-1925) – blurry, hazy, misty, colorful, ambiguous (tonality), evocative, parallel chords (planing), pentatonic and whole-tone scales, irregular meter, small/repeated motives and phrases, poetry, painting, nature, mood over clarity, extreme ranges of pitch and dynamics.
Major Keyboard Composers: Debussy, Ravel.

20th CENTURY / CONTEMPORARY (c. 1900-present) – experimental, percussive, complex, electronic, dissonant, atonal, asymmetrical rhythms, changing meters, twelve-tone, serialism, eclectic, diverse formal structures, specific performing directions, individual, folk melodies, global influences.
Major Keyboard Composers: Bartók, Prokofiev.

PHILIP LOW is a piano teacher in Arden Hills, Minnesota, where he maintains a private studio of nearly 50 students. His students have won numerous competitions, including the MMTA state, Young Artist, Northstar Concerto, Piano Fun, and Saint Paul Piano Teachers contests. An active member of MMTA, Dr. Low has volunteered on the convention committee, exam syllabus committee, and foundation board. He has given lectures at the state convention as well as to local music teacher groups. He holds a Masters and Doctorate in piano performance from the Cleveland Institute of Music as well as a Bachelor of Music from Bethel University in St. Paul.

SONYA SCHUMANN received her D.M.A. and M.M. in piano performance and pedagogy from the University of Michigan and a B.M. from the University of South Carolina. She has performed throughout the United States, Canada, Europe, and Australia, and with orchestras across North America, winning top prizes in several competitions. Active in the artistic community, she also serves as an ambassador for the Piano Arts Consortium, performing benefit concerts and giving masterclasses across the East Coast. She has appeared as guest lecturer and masterclass presenter at several festivals and colleges, including Keys Fest, Music Teachers National Association, Central Michigan University, Red Rocks Music Festival, and Art at Noon at LexArts. She has served as faculty at Madonna University and Schoolcraft College. Dr. Schumann has been on the Levine Music School faculty since 2015, teaching group piano classes and private piano.

CHARMAINE SIAGIAN is editor of Willis publications at Hal Leonard Corporation. She received her D.M.A. in piano performance and pedagogy from the University of Oklahoma and her B.M. and M.M. in piano performance from the Dana School of Music at Youngstown State University. Dr. Siagian has served on the piano faculties of Youngstown State University and Mid-America Christian University, teaching classes in applied and group piano, music theory and history, as well as accompanying chamber choirs, musical theater, and opera workshops. Growing up on North Borneo, her first piano book—perhaps fortuitously—was by John Thompson.